W9-AAX-456

4/03

The California
Missions

Valerie J. Weber and Dale Anderson

Gareth Stevens Publishing
A WORLD ALMANAC EDUCATION GROUP COMPANY

Please visit our web site at: www.garethstevens.com
For a free color catalog describing Gareth Stevens Publishing's list of high-quality
books and multimedia programs, call 1-800-542-2595 (USA) or 1-800-387-3178
(Canada). Gareth Stevens Publishing's fax: (414) 332-3567.

Library of Congress Cataloging-in-Publication Data

Weber, Valerie.
    The California missions / by Valerie J. Weber and Dale Anderson.
      p. cm. — (Events that shaped America)
    Summary: Describes the history of the Spanish missions in California and their effect
on the life of the Indians there.
    Includes bibliographical references and index.
    ISBN 0-8368-3223-X (lib. bdg.)
    1. Indians of North America—Missions—California—Juvenile literature. 2. Missions—
California—Juvenile literature. [1. Indians of North America—California. 2. Missions—
California. 3. California—History.] I. Anderson, Dale, 1953- II. Title. III. Series.
    E78.C15W444   2002
    979.4'02—dc21   2002067027

This North American edition first published in 2002 by
Gareth Stevens Publishing
A World Almanac Education Group Company
330 West Olive Street, Suite 100
Milwaukee, WI 53212 USA

This edition © 2002 by Gareth Stevens Publishing.

Produced by Discovery Books
Editor: Valerie J. Weber
Designer and page production: Sabine Beaupré
Photo researcher: Sabrina Crewe
Maps and diagrams: Stefan Chabluk
Gareth Stevens editorial direction: Mark J. Sachner
Gareth Stevens art direction: Tammy Gruenewald
Gareth Stevens production: Susan Ashley

Photo credits: Corbis: pp. 15, 17, 18, 19, 23, 25, 26, 27; Granger Collection: cover,
pp. 11, 12; Library of Congress: pp. 5 (top), 7, 8, 22; North Wind Picture Archives:
pp. 5 (bottom), 9, 10, 16, 20, 24; Northwestern University Library: p. 6.

Printed in the United States of America

1 2 3 4 5 6 7 8 9 06 05 04 03 02

Contents

Introduction

Who Built the Mission Buildings?

Along California's coast stands a string of twenty-one buildings, most of them over two hundred years old. Built by Native Americans directed by Spanish **friars**, each of these **missions** once included a church, housing, and workshops, but over time, many fell into decay. Today, these missions have been rebuilt and open their doors to people curious about their rich history.

 ## What Happened to the Native Americans?

When the Spanish came, about 300,000 Native Americans were living in California. Unfortunately, the Spanish brought diseases such as measles and smallpox. These diseases were common in Europe, where many people had built up an **immunity** to them. The Native Americans had no such protection, and between 1770 and the 1840s, half of them died from these diseases. The mission system itself killed thousands of Natives as it forced them into harsh labor and terrible living conditions.

The Americans brought trouble as well. In 1848, James Marshall discovered gold at Sutter's Mill. Within months, "gold fever" struck thousands, who rushed to California. The **prospectors** often killed any Natives they found; thousands may have died this way. Others died of disease or causes related to poor food, housing, and treatment. By 1900, fewer than sixteen thousand Native Americans lived in the state of California.

Until the mid-1700s, only Native Americans lived throughout what is now called California. Then, the Spanish Empire spread from Mexico and the Southwest into California. To settle this area, Spain allowed Catholic friars to establish missions. Spanish friars and soldiers forced Native Americans to build the missions and farm the surrounding area.

This drawing appeared in Christopher Columbus's story about his arrival in the Americas. It was published in 1494.

The first mission in California was founded at San Diego. A statue of the mission's founder, Father Junípero Serra, stands in the grounds.

Chapter One

The Native People of California

California's Native Peoples

Before the Spanish came, many different Native American groups lived in different parts of California and traded with each other and with tribes across North America. In northwestern California, groups such as the Yurok and Hupa cut trees from the forests and used them to build houses and canoes. In the northeast, the Modoc and Pomo wove a reed called tule into boats, mats, and coverings for their homes.

Because a lot of foods grew in central California, many Native groups, including the Miwoki, Maidu, and Yuki, lived there. Some groups gathered in villages of nearly one thousand people. The Costanoan and Salinan peoples lived along the central coast and later moved to the missions.

The Chumash, Diegueños, and Tongva stayed along the southern coast, where most missions were built. Fish and plants from the ocean provided much of their food.

Like other Native Californian tribes, the Pomo Indians used tule for many things, including building boats.

Many Native cultures in California made baskets woven in beautiful designs. They used them for practical purposes such as storing food and sorting grain.

Foods

Native Californians were hunters and gatherers who lived off the wild plants and animals. Because much of California was fertile land, people could usually stay in one area year-round. Men hunted and fished, while women gathered nuts, berries, tule, and other plants for food. In good years, they could gather more than they needed and store it for later years. Salmon, plentiful in the rivers flowing to the Pacific Ocean, provided protein for many Native groups. Acorns were also an important source of protein; they could be ground into a coarse flour for baking or cooked as a cereal.

In the hot deserts of the southeast, the Yuma people found only piñon nuts, mesquite beans, and small animals for food. Because there were not as many natural foods in the desert, the Yuma people, unlike other Californian groups, were also farmers. In the northeast, another area with less plentiful food, peoples such as the Modoc and Achumawi ate tule bulbs.

Chapter Two

The Spanish Empire

The Aztecs presented this map of Tenochtitlán to Hernán Cortés between 1519 and 1521. With its huge buildings, the Aztec capital housed over 300,000 people.

Gold and Glory

Like many European countries during the 1400s and 1500s, Spain set out to seek wealth in other lands, sending explorers to North, South, and Central America. In 1519, Hernán Cortés and his men entered the Aztec capital of Tenochtitlán in central Mexico and called it the most beautiful city in the world. Within a decade, the city lay in ruins. The Spaniards tore down public buildings, filled in canals, burned the gardens, and destroyed the Aztecs' religious statues, putting up Christian statues instead. Conquering the Aztec people weakened from European diseases, the Spanish soldiers gained great wealth for themselves and Spain.

In the 1530s, Francisco Pizarro conquered the Incan Empire of South America. He captured the ruler Atahualpa, hoping to exchange him for gold. Once the Incas gave him the gold, Pizarro had Atahualpa killed and seized the Incas' land, mines, storehouses, and temples.

Moving beyond Mexico and South America

The Spanish pushed north from Mexico and Peru and started new **colonies** in what are now Florida and New Mexico. However, Mexico, South America, and the Caribbean remained central to the rich Spanish Empire.

What made the Spanish Empire wealthy was the work of the Native Americans. The Spanish turned the Natives into slaves, forcing them into mines to hack out gold and silver and making them labor on farms and ranches with little food and no pay. They often punished them with whippings, beatings, and death. Sickness, too, took a heavy toll.

The Spanish settled Santa Fe, New Mexico, in 1609. The building shown here is believed to be the oldest Spanish building in the United States.

A Room of Gold

"They led us to our quarters, which were in some large house. . . . Here Montezuma [the Aztec emperor] now kept the great shrines of his gods, and a secret chamber containing gold bars and jewels. This was the treasure which he had inherited from his father, which he had never touched."

Bernal Díaz, a soldier in Cortés's expedition, in his account The True History of the Conquest of New Spain, *written in the 1500s but not published until 1632*

Competing for Power

Other European countries, seeing Spain's success in the Americas, also wanted to gain colonies and riches of their own. As other countries' power in North America grew, Spain wanted to make sure it kept its empire, including the western end of the continent.

Spain hoped to do so by starting settlements north of Mexico. However, few people were willing to move from established Mexican colonies to the land that would become New Mexico, Arizona, and Texas. So Spain decided to send small groups of soldiers and a few friars to these areas to found missions. The friars hoped to **convert** the Native Americans to both Christianity and the Spanish way of life. By the mid-1700s, the friars and soldiers had forced the Natives to build a few missions in this area.

Spain Claims California

Although Spain had claimed the area that is now California in the 1540s, it had done little to settle the land. In the 1750s, however, Russian fur traders began moving into the waters off the coast of northern California. Spain wanted to make sure Russia would not grab the land for itself.

Spain's king ordered Mexico to defend the Spanish Empire, including California, from all other groups, especially Russia. A colonial official in Mexico, José de Gálvez, had wanted to organize all the lands north of Mexico into one large area. The king's orders now gave him that chance.

José de Gálvez's Plan

Gálvez decided to use missions to colonize the lands north of Mexico, including California. The Catholic Church would pay for the friars and the supplies for the missions, saving the Spanish government money. As they had in New Mexico,

As a young man, Junípero Serra rose quickly in the Catholic Church, becoming a teacher in Spain by age twenty-four. However, his real goal was to set up missions in the Americas. In 1749, Serra was sent to Mexico, but it was not until 1768 that he could finally fulfill his goal of beginning missions.

Today, people view Serra in different ways. To many, he is a hero for devoting his energy, mind, and faith to the missions. To others, though, he is someone who was willing to destroy the cultures and religions of Native Americans to impose his own culture and faith on them.

Texas, and Arizona, the friars would convert Native Americans in California to both Christianity and the Spanish culture. Once that was done, it was thought, Mexicans might be more likely to move into the area.

Gálvez had heard that the areas of California where Monterey and San Diego now stand had good harbors and would be excellent spots to place the missions. Ships could easily land, bringing supplies to the friars and soldiers. Two volunteers would lead the trip: the military leader Don Gaspár de Portolá and the religious leader, a friar named Junípero Serra.

Brief Report on the Destruction of the Indians
"To these quiet Lambs [the Native Americans] . . . came the Spaniards like most cruel tigers, wolves, and lions, enraged with a sharp and tedious hunger; for these forty years past, minding nothing else but the slaughter of these unfortunate wretches, whom with diverse kinds of torments neither seen nor heard of before, they have so cruelly and inhumanely butchered."

Spanish priest Bartolomé de las Casas in a 1542 report about the treatment of Indians by the Spanish

Chapter Three

Starting the Missions

Father Serra watches as soldiers place a cross to mark the founding of the first California mission in July 1769.

The First California Missions

In early 1769, four different groups with more than two hundred men left Mexico by land and by sea. All were to meet at today's San Diego. Though their directions and the weather were poor, members of all four groups reached the right area in early July.

Unfortunately, about half the men had died or deserted in the process. However, Father Serra celebrated **Mass** with the remaining men and claimed the site for the first California mission, San Diego de Alcalá.

Over the next months, some of the Spaniards built a crude church and shelters at San Diego, while others, led by Portolá, searched unsuccessfully for the harbor now called Monterey. The mission at San Diego was losing men rapidly to disease. There had also been conflict with the Tipai Indians, who were angry that the Spanish had moved into their area. Food was scarce, and Serra had not made a single convert.

The Presidios

In March 1770, the Spaniards were saved when a ship arrived with supplies. Portolá, back from looking for Monterey, built a presidio, or small fort, near the mission. He then left to search again for the harbor at Monterey. Serra and another friar were to meet him there by ship.

This time, Portolá found Monterey, where Serra met him a few days later. On June 3, 1770, Serra founded the second California mission—San Carlos Borroméo de Carmelo. The same day, near the mission, Portolá founded the presidio of Monterey.

A Chain of Missions

Father Serra and the other friars continued to found missions over the next fifteen years. After Serra died in 1784, Fermín Francisco de Lasuén, who had run the San Diego mission, took over his job. Between 1785 and 1803, Lasuén oversaw the beginnings of nine more missions. After Lasuén died, three more missions were added to the chain. The last two extended that chain north of the present-day city of San Fancisco.

Presidios

While the missions were put on rich crop land, presidios were built where they could best protect missions from Native American groups in case of a fight. For food, the few soldiers in the presidios depended on the missions and the small towns, or pueblos, that grew up nearby. Besides the ones at San Diego and Monterey, presidios were built at San Francisco and Santa Barbara.

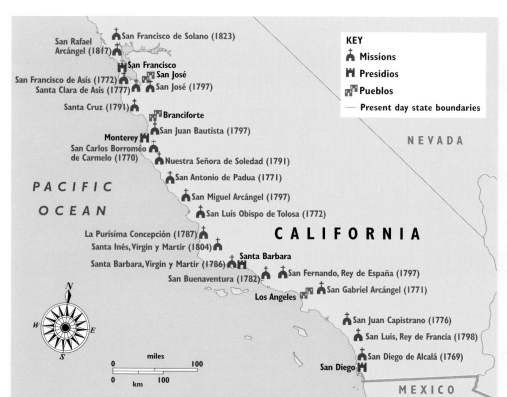

KEY

✝ 🏠 **Missions**

🏰 **Presidios**

🏛 **Pueblos**

— **Present day state boundaries**

San Francisco de Solano (1823)
San Rafael Arcángel (1817)
San Francisco
San Francisco de Asís (1772)
San José
San José (1797)
Santa Clara de Asís (1777)
Santa Cruz (1791)
Branciforte
San Juan Bautista (1797)
Monterey
San Carlos Borroméo de Carmelo (1770)
Nuestra Señora de Soledad (1791)
San Antonio de Padua (1771)
San Miguel Arcángel (1797)
San Luis Obispo de Tolosa (1772)
La Purísima Concepción (1787)
Santa Inés, Virgin y Martir (1804)
Santa Barbara, Virgin y Martir (1786)
Santa Barbara
San Buenaventura (1782)
San Fernando, Rey de España (1797)
San Gabriel Arcángel (1771)
Los Angeles
San Juan Capistrano (1776)
San Luis, Rey de Francia (1798)
San Diego de Alcalá (1769)
San Diego

PACIFIC OCEAN

CALIFORNIA

NEVADA

MEXICO

N W E S

miles
0   100
0   100
km

By 1823, a chain of missions stretched along the southern and central California coast from San Diego to north of today's San Francisco.

This diagram shows how typical missions were built around a central courtyard. Networks of ditches carried water to orchards, fields, gardens, and mission buildings.

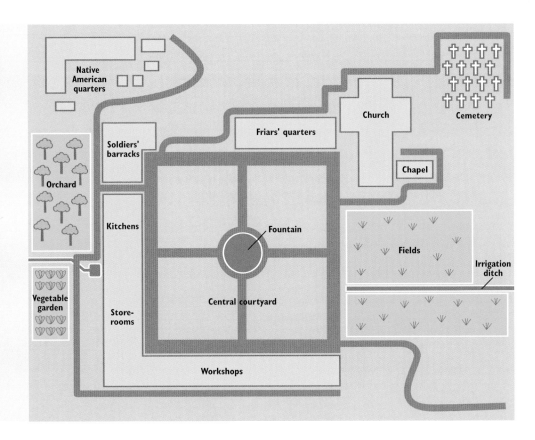

Native American quarters

Church

Cemetery

Friars' quarters

Soldiers' barracks

Orchard

Chapel

Kitchens

Fountain

Fields

Irrigation ditch

Vegetable garden

Store-rooms

Central courtyard

Workshops

Building the Missions

The friars tried to put the missions far enough apart so that they would have different groups of Native people to convert and to use for workers. They chose fertile land with water nearby, land that would make good farmland.

Forced into labor by the friars, Natives built the first missions of wood with straw for the roof. When Native groups shot flaming arrows at the buildings, however, the straw caught fire easily. The friars soon had their roofs constructed with tiles made of baked earth. These red tiles became a well-known part of mission **architecture** across California.

As the missions became more successful, the buildings became more permanent; **stucco** covered their **adobe** walls. Missions grew to include a church, housing for the friars and workers, storehouses, kitchens, and workshops.

The Missions Grow

The friars also built *asistencias,* which were on mission lands some miles from the church and other buildings. Asistencias had no chapel or live-in friars, but priests came from the missions to say Mass and perform marriages and funerals. Some asistencias were supposed to become missions.

The Spanish also established a few towns, known as pueblos, to supply the presidios with food. The government offered free land, animals, and farm supplies to anyone (including Native people) who would settle at the pueblos. In return, the settlers sold their crops to the soldiers living at the presidios.

Walls of Clay

In the brickyard at the Santa Barbara mission today lie rows of adobe bricks, used in building the missions' thick walls. The bricks were formed in wooden molds from clay, water, manure, and straw and then baked in the sun. The bricks were very heavy, about 60 pounds (27 kilograms) each, so mission walls had to be thick to bear their own weight. Santa Barbara today still sports its famous red tile roof.

Chapter Four

Mission Life

Friars and Soldiers

Two Franciscan friars ran each mission. (Franciscans were members of a **Roman Catholic** order of priests.) One was responsible for religious life and one oversaw the work. Sometimes they switched jobs. They totally controlled the lives and work of the people living at the missions.

About five or six soldiers usually protected each mission and made sure the workers did their jobs. If an emergency arose in a mission, the soldiers sent for help from one of the four presidios. During the mission period, only a few hundred soldiers lived in California.

The friars ruled at the missions, not only over the Native workers but also over the soldiers living there. Here, soldiers interrupt their card game to show respect to the friar.

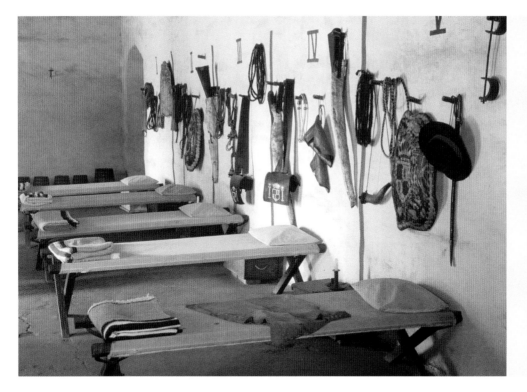

Soldiers stayed in **barracks** in or near the mission. This barrack at La Purísima mission has been rebuilt to show visitors how the soldiers lived.

Making Converts

The friars at the California missions had two goals: to convert Native people and to enrich the missions and thus the Spanish Empire. Spain had given the missions nearly unlimited land; the missions needed the free labor of the Indians to work it. The friars forced the Natives to learn farming and craft skills that would support the missions and make money for the Spanish Empire.

 A Trick to Convert

The friars made converts, called "**neophytes**," in several ways. Sometimes they offered people gifts or food to convert. Sometimes they used tricks. One trick was to **baptize** a child, making him or her a Christian, then keep the child from the parents until they decided to become Christian as well.

California Indians wearing body paint perform a traditional dance. The friars tried to stop the Native Americans' traditional practices such as dancing.

Why Did the Indians Convert?

Of course, the Native Americans the friars were trying to convert had their own strong religious beliefs and practices. The two groups also held quite different beliefs about religion itself. The friars thought the Natives should convert completely to Christianity, giving up all their Native religions. The Native Americans felt they could use some Christian **symbols** and **rituals** in the practice of their own traditional religion, without changing their basic beliefs. As a result, while many Natives participated in Christian rituals, such as allowing themselves to be baptized, they still practiced their traditional religion.

Oddly enough, the diseases that nearly wiped out Native Americans also pushed some of them into converting. Natives saw their people dying of diseases such as measles while the Spanish, having immunity to those diseases, did not. Perhaps Christianity itself might contain the power to help them resist the diseases. Some converted, hoping to stay healthy.

Most friars learned little about Native languages and religions. Those who did, though, learned to use Native symbols and beliefs to explain Christian symbols and beliefs,

Herded into the Missions

As time passed, fewer Native Americans wanted to convert or work at the missions. Sometimes, soldiers simply rounded them up and forced them into the missions. By 1800, a total of thirteen thousand people lived at the missions; the numbers at each mission ranged from a few hundred to three thousand.

making it easier for the Natives to understand and convert. This way, friars converted some Indians gradually from their Native religion to Christianity.

Everyday Life

Most of the Native Americans slaved in the fields, growing many crops, including wheat, corn, beans, chickpeas, other vegetables, and fruits. They also raised cattle and sheep. As the missions grew and cattle ranching became important, outlying ranches called *estancias* were built. Native workers lived on the ranches with a Spanish overseer who directed their work.

These people are working at a mission. The people on the left are weaving baskets, while the ones in the middle are spinning rope.

When Lasuén took over from Serra, he forced male mission residents to learn metalwork, woodwork, tanning, and stonecutting. Women made woolen cloth into clothing for people at the missions and the presidios. From mission cattle and crops, they made soap, candles, and wine. And of course, they continued to raise the children and cook the meals.

The Indians toiled from dawn to dusk, with very little food and under the constant threat of whipping or other punishment. The food they received was much less than that given to the friars or soldiers. At nights, families with small children slept in small huts, but older children and single adults were packed into smelly, ill-lit buildings, one for women and one for men.

A mission resident sits high up in the bell tower to ring the bells. Bells called the Indians to prayers, meals, and work.

A Harsh Life

Although the friars were religious, they used violence to control the Natives and force them to work. The friars thought the Natives were "uncivilized" and thus did not have to be treated like other people. Beatings were common, as was chaining people and forcing them to work with heavy weights on their feet. The friars, soldiers, and their assistants whipped the

Natives for the slightest offense or put them in the **stocks**. While some friars and missions were better than others, many treated Native Americans like slaves.

Resisting and Escaping the Missions

Soon after San Diego de Alcalá was begun, a group of Tipai Indians attacked, but the Spanish fought them off. In 1824, a group of Chumash Indians seized the missions of Santa Inés and La Purísima Concepción and defended them for nearly a month. Soldiers from the presidio at Monterey finally defeated the rebels.

As the missions grew, Natives rebelled in other ways as well. In a few cases, they killed the friars who had treated them so harshly for so long. Many tried to leave the missions and return to their old lives or other villages. About 10 percent of all mission Natives fled each year; at Santa Barbara mission, however, that number increased to 15 percent. Sometimes a few hundred Natives escaped at once and hid as far as they could from the soldiers chasing them. If they were caught, they were whipped or put in the stocks.

Life by the Bell

"The Indians at the mission of Santa Cruz, after prayers in the morning at church, received their orders as to their labors at the church door; then they went to breakfast. . . . At eleven a.m., the bell was rung to call them together. . . . The dinner consisted of cooked horse beans and peas. At the end of an hour the bell was rung again, and all went to work until about sunset, when each received his rations of boiled corn."

Lorenzo Asisaro, a mission resident remembering life at Santa Cruz mission, 1877

Strokes of a Whip

"In a word, everything reminded us of a . . . West Indian [slave] colony. . . . We mention it with pain. The resemblance is so perfect, that we saw men and women loaded with irons, others in the stocks; and at length the noise of the strokes of a whip struck our ears."

Jean Francois Galaup de La Perouse, who visited Mission San Carlos Borroméo while on a scientific exploration for the French government in the late 1700s

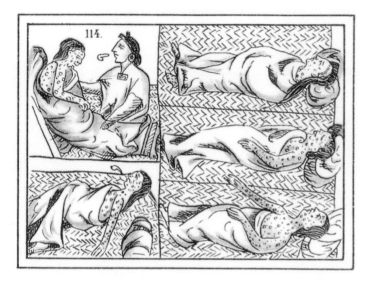

A People Reduced, an Empire Increased

Mission life was brutal for the Native Americans. Underfed, overworked, and crowded into unhealthy living spaces, they fell victim to disease by the thousands. The aged, the very young, and pregnant women died most frequently; in 1820, 86 percent of the children born at the missions died as babies.

With their slave labor, the California missions made a great deal of money. By the 1830s, the Indians were raising hundreds of thousands of cattle and sheep and thousands of horses. The missions used some of the food, wool, and hides they produced themselves and traded the rest with merchants who stopped along the coast to pick up these products.

Success helped them grow. At one time, the missions owned one-sixth of California.

Why They Fled

"He had been [whipped] for leaving without permission."
"He was frightened at seeing how his friends were always being flogged."
"When he wept over the death of his wife and children, he was ordered whipped five times."
"His mother, two brothers, and three nephews died, all of hunger, and he ran away so that he would not also die."

Reasons given by a group of Indians for running away from San Francisco de Asís mission in 1797

Mission Production

"The products of the mission are butter, **tallow**, hides, chamois [goat] leather, bear skins, wine, white wine, brandy, oil, corn, wheat, beans also bull horns which the English take by the thousand."

Mission Indian Pablo Tac, describing the mission
San Luis Rey de Francia, 1835

The mission of San Carlos Borroméo de Carmelo was founded in 1770. It was soon moved from Monterey to the fertile Carmel Valley. There, the mission was rebuilt in stone and became the headquarters of the mission system in California.

The Mission Era Ends

A Plan to Disband

Although the missions created wealth, Spain never meant them to continue forever. The friars were supposed to move on to establish other missions and priests were to run only the church. In the 1830s, the government finally came up with a plan. The mission land would be divided among the neophytes, who would become loyal subjects of Spain. Government officials were to look after half the livestock and equipment until the mission became a pueblo. The other half was to be divided among the neophytes. The Catholic Church would keep the church, the friars' rooms, and the vegetable gardens.

In reality, none of this happened. The government officials sent to look after the land until it had been divided sold most

A Change in Government and Ideas

By the 1820s, Mexico was independent of Spain, and California was a Mexican province. The California missions were losing their residents; more people were dying there than being born. There were fewer people to do the hard work of raising crops and animals and producing goods to trade. Finally, in 1834, the Mexican government decided to break up the missions and divide their fertile lands and animals.

Long after the missions had been deserted, this kitchen at the Carmel mission was restored to how it looked originally.

of it to their friends, family, and local businessmen. Some Native Americans did get the land, but most lost it or sold it to white settlers. Soon, most of the Mission Indians were without a home or land, forced to take any job they could find. They became low-paid workers for the growing Hispanic and Anglo population or they fled into other tribes and settlements.

The Missions Decay

With the friars and neophytes gone, the missions fell apart. People took materials from the churches to build their homes and farm buildings. The nonreligious buildings were turned into homes, stores, farms, and stables for the new owners.

Weather took its toll as well; roof timbers and walls rotted and collapsed. Within a short time, most of the missions were ruins. Earthquakes also destroyed a few of them.

During the mid- to late 1800s, a few mission churches remained open, but most were neglected. Artists often sketched or painted the ruins, and by the early 1900s, their work began to attract interest. Soon railroad companies were putting together tours of the old missions for tourists.

During the 1900s, various California groups rebuilt the missions. Some missions look nothing like they did originally, while others are faithful to their original design.

Conclusion

Today

Now all the missions are rebuilt and are open to visitors. The Catholic Church again owns two-thirds of the missions and holds religious services in them. Two of the missions are California State historical parks, where visitors can learn about early mission life.

Today the Franciscan order still owns and runs the mission at San Antonio de Padua.

 El Camino Reál

To connect the missions, the Spanish forced local Native Americans to build the first road in California, called *El Camino Reál*, or "the Royal Road." It was not much more than a wide dirt track that stretched nearly 600 miles (965 kilometers) from San Diego in the south to Sonoma in the north. Curving around the mountains, its route made so much sense that today's highways run along the same path.

It's hard to believe when you look at this beautiful and peaceful court-yard at San Juan Capistrano that the missions were once places of such misery.

Looking Back

The time of the missions brought huge changes to California. The culture changed from Native American to European. While the missions did not fully convert all the Native Americans to Christianity or to a Spanish way of life, they did plant Spanish culture in the area. The missions also encouraged European-style farming and brought cattle ranching and sheep herding to the area. Of course, Spanish culture could gain strength because so many Native Americans died from European diseases or were killed by the Spanish, Mexicans, or Americans.

In the late 1840s, English-speaking settlers came to California by the thousands, outnumbering the few Spanish-speakers. Still, evidence of the Spanish culture remains in California's buildings, language, foods, religion, music, arts, and businesses.

Time Line

1519	Hernán Cortés enters Aztec capital in central Mexico.
1530s	Francisco Pizarro conquers Incan Empire of South America.
1609	Spanish settle what is now Santa Fe, New Mexico.
mid-1700s	Spanish start missions in today's New Mexico, Arizona, and Texas.
1769	Don Gaspár de Portolá and Father Junípero Serra lead a group of men to settle California and found the first mission, San Diego de Alcalá, and first presidio at San Diego.
1770	Serra starts Mission San Carlos de Borroméo de Carmel, and Portolá begins presidio at Monterey.
1771–1782	Seven more missions are begun under Serra's leadership.
1784	Serra dies.
1785	Father Fermín Francisco de Lasuén is named to lead the California missions.
1821	Mexico gains independence from Spain, and California becomes a Mexican province.
1823	Last mission, San Francisco de Solano, is founded.
1824	Chumash Indians revolt and seize missions of Santa Inés and La Purísima Concepción.
1834	Mexican government orders the breaking up of the missions.
1848	James Marshall discovers gold at Sutter's Mill in California.
1857	An earthquake destroys Mission Santa Cruz.
1868	An earthquake destroys Mission San José.
1879	Work begins to restore Mission San Fernando, Rey de España.
1926	An electrical fire destroys Mission Santa Clara de Asís.
1941	Restoration of La Purísima Concepción is completed.
1982–1985	San José becomes the last mission to be rebuilt.

Things to Think About and Do

Why Do People Live Where They Do?

Before the Spanish came to California, most Native Americans lived where there was a good supply of food growing and animals to be hunted. The Spanish put their missions and pueblos where there were good harbors and fertile land to farm.

Look at a map of the United States or of your state that shows where people live today. Where do most people live now? Why do you think they live there? Why is a supply of food growing in an area no longer an important reason to live there?

A Different Life

Imagine what your life would be like if you were a Native American living in California when the Spanish came. What would it feel like to be made to live in a completely different way, to wear different clothes, eat different foods, and believe different ideas?

Two Views

See if you can find artists' drawings of an old, tumbledown mission and draw one yourself. Then imagine what that mission must have looked like when it was busiest in the early 1800s and draw a picture of the mission, the friars, soldiers, and workers.

Glossary

adobe: building material made of mud mixed with straw.

architecture: style or way of building houses and other structures.

baptize: make a person a Christian with a naming ceremony.

barrack: housing for soldiers.

colony: settlement, area, or country owned or controlled by another nation.

convert: cause a person to change a belief, usually a religious one.

friar: priest who belongs to a Catholic religious order.

immunity: protection from a disease.

Mass: main religious ceremony in the Roman Catholic Church.

mission: center built by Spanish in the American Southwest and California to convert Native Americans to Christianity and exploit their labor.

neophyte: person who has recently changed his or her religious beliefs.

order: group of people who live under the same rules or belong to the same organization.

prospector: person who explores an area looking for valuable resources such as gold or oil.

ritual: system of special ceremonies in a religion.

Roman Catholic: relating to a Christian church whose members recognize the Pope in Rome, Italy, as their supreme leader.

stocks: device for punishing people. A person's head and hands are placed through holes in a wooden structure and locked into place. The person is then left for a long time.

stucco: mixture of cement, sand, and powdered limestone used to cover walls.

symbol: something that stands for or represents something else.

tallow: animal fat—usually taken from cattle, sheep, or horses—used to make candles or soap.

Further Information

Books

Abbink, Emily. *Missions of the Monterey Bay Area* (*California Missions*). Lerner Publications, 1997.

Brower, Pauline. *Missions of the Inland Valleys* (*California Missions*). Lerner Publications, 1997.

Fraser, Mary Ann. *A Mission for the People: La Purísima.* Henry Holt & Company, 1998.

Schwabacher, Martin. *The Chumash Indians* (*The Junior Library of American Indians*). Chelsea House, 1995.

Web Sites

www.ca-missions.org Large collection of information about California missions.

library.thinkquest.org/3615/ Information about California missions, including a tour of a typical mission, and the people who lived in them.

www.notfrisco.com/almanac/missions/ Old photographs of all the California missions with information on each and a collection of historical papers.

Useful Addresses

La Purísima Mission State Historic Park
California State Parks
2295 Purísima Road
Lompoc, CA 93436
Telephone: (805) 733-3713

Carmel Mission Basilica
Rio Road and Lasuén Drive,
Carmel, CA 93921
Telephone: (831) 624-3600

Index

Page numbers in **bold** indicate pictures.